Bryn Mawr Latin Commentaries

Editors

Julia Haig Gaisser
Bryn Mawr College

James J. O'Donnell
University of Pennsylvania

D1604059

The purpose of the Bryn Mawr Latin Commentaries is to make a wide range of classical and post-classical authors accessible to the intermediate student. Each commentary provides the minimum grammatical and lexical information necessary for a first reading of the text.

Bryn Mawr Latin Commentaries

Prudentius

Psychomachia

COMMENTARY

Rosemary Burton

Copyright ©1989 by Bryn Mawr College

Manufactured in the United States of America

ISBN: 0-929524-61-6

Printed and distributed by:
    Bryn Mawr Commentaries
    Thomas Library
    Bryn Mawr College
    Bryn Mawr, PA 19010

COMMENTARY

Preface

In the preface, Prudentius gives a short preview of the theme of the work as a whole a spiritual battle ending in the triumph of virtue. He does this by retelling and interpretation of some events in the life of Abraham. By the time P. wrote, allegorical methods of interpreting the Bible were well established. Old Testament characters and events were seen as foreshadowing or "prefiguring" events in the life of Christ, the Church or the individual Christian. The process had already begun in the New Testament authors; Paul's letter to the Galatians (4.21-31) provides a good example.

1-14. Statement of theme: the life of Abraham provides an example of the battles of the Christian life. Lines 1-14 are a single complex sentence; the subject is *Abram*.

1-2. Senex ... via ... pater: nouns in apposition to *Abram*.

credendi: gerund.

2. beati seminis: Cf. Genesis 22.18 "et benedicentur in semine tuo omnes gentes terrae." The phrase has several layers of meaning, referring primarily to Abraham's son Isaac, and through him to the Jewish people and perhaps also to Christ and the Christians.

serus: i.e. late in life.

3. cuius: introduces relative clause.

adiecta ... syllaba: nominatives, subject of relative clause. **adiecta:** perfect participle < *adicio*, "add."

auxit: perfect < *augeo*, "increase."

4. Abram parenti ... Abraham deo: Genesis 17.5. "No longer shall your name be Abram, but your name shall be Abraham ..." *parenti ... deo:* datives of agent dependent on the participle *dictus*, "called."

5. senile: "of his old age"; (cf. line 1, *senex*, line 2, *serus*).

pignus: here, "child."

dicauit: < *dico, -are,* "dedicate."

uictimae: dative of purpose. The story of Abraham's sacrifice of Isaac is told in Genesis 22.1-19.

6. **docens:** governs indirect statement introduced by *quod* (7).

cum: introduces a subordinate clause within the indirect statement.

ad aram: include in *cum* clause.

litare: "to sacrifice," intransitive.

quis: indefinite pronoun, "anyone."

7. **quod . . . unicum:** Translate *quod* as "what" and supply *sit.* These three elliptical relative clauses provide the subject for the infinitive *offerendum (esse).*

pium: "beloved."

unicum: Cf. Genesis 22.16; "because you have done this, and have not withheld your son, your only son . . ."

8. **deo . . . credito:** ablative absolute. Cf. *credendi* in line 1.

9. **pugnare:** complementary infinitive dependent on both *suasit* and *exemplum dedit.*

nosmet: "us" (emphatic).

profanis gentibus: "gentiles, pagans"; used allegorically of the vices which attack the soul.

10. **suasit . . . dedit:** These are the main verbs in the sentence. *suasit:* perfect < *suadeo,* "persuade"; *suasor,* "persuader" from the same root.

11. **nec** = *et non.* The construction changes abruptly. The accusative and infinitive *pugnare nosmet* expresses a command; but *nec* introduces a further idea which is expressed not as an exhortation but as a fact in indirect statement, "and that we do not . . ."

ante: with *quam* (14) = *antequam.*

coniugalem: "legitimate," like Isaac in contrast to Ishmael, Abraham's elder son by a slave-woman.

12. **matre:** in apposition to *uirtute,* "as a mother."

editam: perfect participle < *edo, edere,* "bring forth."

13. **strage:** ablative < *strages,* "slaughter."

multa: ablative.

14. **portenta:** "monsters."

seruientis: present participle, "being a slave, enslaved." Part of the soul, the *cor* (heart, mind) is enslaved to vice until rescued by another part, the *spiritus.*

uicerit: perfect subjunctive < *uinco* (subordinate clause in indirect statement).

15-49. Central narrative section of the Preface, based on Genesis chs. 14 and 18.

15-37. In Genesis 14, an alliance of Eastern kings conquers the wealthy cities of Sodom and Gomorrah. Among their prisoners is Abram's nephew Lot. Abram, with a small force of his own servants, routs the kings' army and rescues Lot.

15. uictum: perfect participle < *uinco*, modifies *Loth*.

16. Loth: accusative, indeclinable in Latin, like many Hebrew names.
inmorantem: < *inmoror* "linger in."

17. aduena: "as an immigrant," in apposition to the understood subject, "he."

18. pollens: < *polleo*, "be powerful, important."
patruelis: genitive, adjective derived < *patruus*, "uncle," hence, "of his uncle's."

19. sinistris ... nuntiis: dative of the agent with the perfect participle *excitatus*. Take *nuntiis* to mean "messengers" rather than "news," since Abram does not actually hear the news until the next line. The adjective *sinistris* (unlucky, bad) can quite naturally be extended from the message to the messengers.

20. propinquum: subject of an indirect statement dependent on *audit*.

21. seruire: takes dative.

22. ter: "three times"; *senos:* "six." Latin poets usually resort to periphrasis to avoid such monstrosities as *duodeuigintique*; but the expression of the number 318 in terms of multiples of three is also a hint to the reader to expect some theological significance (for which see on 57-8).
uernulas: diminutive form of *uerna* "a slave born in the household." In late Latin diminutives are commonly used without special significance.

23. pergant ut = *ut pergant*, < *pergo*: "proceed, press on to" (+ dependent infinitive).
hostis: singular instead of the more usual plural, despite plural *terga*.

24. gaza: "treasure."

25. captis ... copiis: ablative of means. *copiis:* "wealth."

26. quin: "moreover, besides."
ipse: Abram.
plenus deo: i.e., divinely inspired.

27. graues: + ablative, "weighed down by."

28. sauciatos: < *saucio,* "wound."

proterit: < *protero,* "trample, crush."

30-1. A list of the plunder follows, in a series of nouns in apposition to *rapinam.*

30. monilia: < *monile,* neuter: "necklace."

31. buculas: < *bucula,* f. "heifer."

32. ruptis . . . nexibus: ablative of separation. *nexibus:* < *nexus,* "bond."

33. attrita: < *attero,* "rub, chafe."

bacis: < *baca,* originally "berry," hence anything small and round, hence "link" of a chain.

34. dissipator: "one who routs," < *dissipo, -are.*

hostici: adjective < *hostis.*

35. recepta prole: ablative of cause depending on *inclytus,* "famous."

fratris: dependent on *prole.*

36. quam: The indefinite pronoun *quis* is commonly used after *si, nisi, ne,* or *num.*

fidelis: genitive; cf. line 1.

prosapiam: "stock, offspring."

38-44. Genesis 14.17-19. "After his return from the defeat of . . . the kings . . . Melchizedek king of Salem brought out bread and wine; he was priest of God Most High. And he blessed him . . ."

38. recentem: modifies *uirum.*

39. donat: here takes ablative of thing given, accusative of person to whom it is given.

ferculis: < *ferculum,* "food, dish."

caelestibus: "heavenly," because of their sacramental overtones.

40. sacerdos: repeated for emphasis.

rex: placed before *et* for emphasis. A more normal word-order would be *sacerdos et idem rex.* Melchizedek's identification with both roles is stressed. While he makes only a brief cameo appearance in Genesis, Melchizedek is important in the Epistle to the Hebrews, whose author interprets his priesthood as a model for the priestly function of Christ (Hebrews 7.1-10).

praepotens: prae + potens, "very powerful."

41. origo: nominative, subject of relative clause introduced by *cuius.*

inenarrabili: "unable to be told, ineffable." The silence of Genesis about Melchizedek's ancestry is taken by the author of Hebrews to imply a mysterious origin, paralleling that of Christ.

42. secreta: nominative with *origo*.

prodit: "reveals, betrays."

sui: "of itself."

43. Melchisedech: nominative, in apposition to *sacerdos*.

qua stirpe, quis maioribus: indirect questions dependent on both *ignotus* and *cognitus*. Understand a verb "to be" or "to be descended from." *quis:* poetic form of *quibus*.

44. ignotus: sc. *hominibus*.

uni: dative modifying *deus*, "alone."

cognitus (+ dative): perfect participle < *cognosco*, "known."

tantum: adverb, "only."

45. mox: P. skips three chapters of Genesis, occupying some considerable span of time, and proceeds to chapter 18, thus suggesting a closer link between the incidents than appears in the original.

triformis: "three-formed, three-bodied." See Genesis 18.1-2, where God appears to Abraham in the form of three men. P. here seems to combine two explanations of this odd apparation: 1) the three men were angels (*angelorum*); 2) they express the trinitarian nature of God (*triformis, trinitas*). See 63 and note.

46. senis: genitive of *senex*, used as an adjective.

mapalia: neuter plural, "huts," a foreign word used for the huts of nomadic people.

47. iam: taken with *uietam* ("aged," modifying *aluum*).

Sarra: Sarah, Abraham's wife.

aluum: < *aluus* (second declension feminine), "womb."

48. munus: "gift, function," object of *stupet*. *munus iuuentae:* "function, gift of youth," i.e., fertility; acc. subj. of an infinitive to be understood (e.g., *uenisse*). The phrase is governed by *stupet*.

mater: in apposition to *Sarra*.

exsanquis: < *ex* + *sanguis*, "bloodless, dried-up, worn-out." The proximity of *stupet* also suggests "pale from shock."

49. herede: albative of cause.

cachinni: < *cachinnus*, "laugh."

paenitens (+ genitive): "sorry for." Sarah's laugh was her first reaction to the news that she would bear a son despite being well past child-bearing age (Genesis 18.11-25).

50-68. P. now explains the allegorical meaning of the narrative, in language which echoes that of the story itself.

50. haec: modifies *linea*, "outline."

figuram: "figure, image."

praenotata: < *prae* + *notare*, "to make a mark beforehand."

51. quam: introduces relative clause of purpose.

recto . . . pede: "with true, accurate measure."

resculpat: < *resculpo*, "carve out again." The metaphor is that of an engraver who first makes an outline drawing and then makes his engraving by following the outline exactly.

52. Indirect statement extending down to 58. The verb introducing it is implied in the previous sentence.

uigilandum: understand *esse*; impersonal use of the gerundive, "one must be vigilant."

53. omnem . . . portionem: accusative subject of the infinitive *liberandam (esse)* (line 55).

54. capta: agrees with *quae* (antecedent *portionem*).

seruiat: subjunctive in subordinate clause in indirect statement.

55. domi: goes closely with *coactis*.

coactis: perfect participle < *cogo*, "collect, recruit."

56. nos . . . diuites: a third indirect statement, conjunction omitted.

large: "abundantly"; take with *diuites*.

uernularum: cf. 22 and note.

diuites (+ genitive): "rich in."

57. quid: introduces indirect question dependent on *nouerimus*.

bis novenis additis: ablative absolute. *nouenis:* "nine." Cf. 22.

58. possint: verb in indirect question, governing *quid*.

figura: ablative, "symbol."

nouerimus: subjunctive verb in indirect statement < *noui*, "know."

mystica: "mystic, mysterious"; modifies *figura*. P. prefers to keep the number mysterious by only hinting at its meaning. In antiquity, numbers were often regarded as having symbolic value. Christian commentators on Genesis had ingeniously interpreted Abram's 318 slaves as a symbol for the crucified Christ. The number would be represented in Greek notation by the letters TIH. T from its shape represents the cross, and IH are the first two letters of the name Jesus in Greek.

59-63. mox . . . hospitae: In his interpretation, P. runs together two incidents which are separate in the narrative. The encounter with

103. baptismate: The Greek verb *baptizein* means "to dip," but the noun *baptisma* is normally used only with the specialized Christian meaning.

labem: "stain."

104. contenta: governs *condere* (see on 40).

piatum: "cleansed"; cf. *expiat* (102).

105. uaginae: dative of motion towards.

rubigo: nominative, "rust."

106. scabrosa: "rough, dirty."

107. catholico: originally meaning "universal," later "orthodox, in accord with the universal church."

diuini fontis: Take with *aram*. In ancient paganism springs and rivers were regarded as divine and might have altars dedicated to them. On the allegorical level, P. is presumably thinking of such texts as John 4.14, *sed aqua, quam ego dabo ei, fiet in eo fons aquae salientis ad uitam aeternam*.

108. ubi . . . coruscet: relative clause of purpose.

109-77. Third combat; battle between Ira and Patientia.

109. graui . . . uultu: ablative of manner.

110. per: "in."

111. rigidis . . . pilis ["javelins"]: dative.

peruia: "penetrable to, pierced by."

112. defixa: perfect participle < *defigo* "cast down."

oculos: accusative of respect.

lenta: "inactive."

113. spumanti . . . rictu: ablative of manner.

114. sanguinea: "bloodshot."

subfuso [< *suffundo*, "cause to well up"] **felle:** ablative describing *lumina*.

115. ut: "as."

exsortem: < *exsors*, "without share or lot in"; takes genitive.

teloque et uoce = et telo et uoce.

116. inpatiens: takes genitive.

conto: < *contus*, "pike, spear."

117. hirsutas: "feathered, plumed."

galeato: "helmeted."

cristas: Translate as singular, "crest."

118. en: a word used to call attention: "hey!"

tibi: dative of reference (more precisely, the ethical dative, that 'faded variety of the Dative of Reference' [*AG* 380]).

Martis: a standard personification in poetry, virtually identical in meaning with *belli*.

libera: here, "taking no part in," with genitive.

119. **securo:** "confident."

120. **turpe:** supply *est*.

dolorem = "a cry of pain," direct object of *gemuisse* (a rare use).

121. **stridens:** "whistling."

pinus: i.e., a spear.

122. **crispata:** < *crispo*, "brandish, shake," here "throw with a quivering motion."

notos: literally, "south winds," but here used generally for any wind.

123. **inliditur:** "is struck"; the passive emphasizes that the spear is only the instrument.

124. **loricae:** "breastplate."

repulsu: "rebound, resistance."

125. **conserto:** perfect participle < *consero*, "fasten together".

adamante: "adamant," a mythical substance known for its extreme hardness; ablative of material.

trilicem: < *trilex*, "with a triple thread."

126. **thoraca:** Greek accusative < *thorax*, "breastplate, cuirass."

squamosa: "scaly"; *squamosa ferri texta:* i.e., chain-mail.

127. **intortos:** < *intorqueo*, "interlace."

conmiserat: < *committo*, "attach."

neruos: "thongs."

129. **non penetrabile:** "impenetrably"; for neuter adjectives used adverbially, cf. line 295 below.

durans: "enduring."

130. **monstri:** i.e., Ira.

sine more: "uncontrollably, ungovernably."

131. **opperiens:** "waiting for" (+ direct object).

132. **stomachando:** ablative of gerund < *stomachor*, "rage."

133. **inpenderat:** "spent," here "exhausted."

134. **superuacuam:** "useless."

inrita: An adjective agreeing with the subject often has virtual adverbial force; translate "vainly."

ignotis . . . ab oris: The foreign origin of Christianity is a cause for suspicion.

230. ius: "right." *ius uindicat:* sc. in the redemption.

exul: An exile lost his right to ownership of property.

231ff. Superbia echoes the arguments of contemporary anti-Christian polemic.

231. nimirum: "of course" (used ironically.)

232. quandoque: indefinite, "at some time or other."

233. solacia: neuter plural nominative.

234. desidiam: "laziness."

rerum: i.e., of the next world.

meditamine: < *meditamen,* "thinking ahead, expectation."

palpent: < *palpo, -are,* "soothe."

235. quidni: "What if not . . ."

palpet: conditional subjunctive.

236. tirones: < *tiro,* "raw recruit."

Bellona: the goddess of war.

aere: ablative < *aes*; here = "trumpet."

237. tepefacta: "cooled, lukewarm."

resoluit: "unnerves."

238. anne = an + ne.

iecur: In antiquity the liver was regarded as the seat of the emotions. Translate "heart."

239. sudatur: "is sweated over."

240. quam: introduces an exclamation (to 248): "how."

Mauors: archaic form of *Mars.*

conscia: "conscious, aware of itself."

241. nugas: "trash."

242. choreis: "dancing-bands."

243. egens: modifies *Iustitia.*

Honestas: "Integrity."

244. albo . . . uultu: ablative of description.

Ieiunia: "Fasting."

245. sanguine: sc. in the cheeks.

interfusus: "suffused, colored" (+ ablative.)

aperta: modifies *Simplicitas.*

246. patens: "exposed"; sc. *Simplicitas.*

247. iudice sese: ablative absolute. *sese* = *se.*

248. degenerem: "as degenerate"; proleptic adjective expressing the effect of the verbal action on the object.

249. faxo: archaic future form of *facio*; introduces a result clause.
stipularum: "straw."
more: "in the manner of," i.e., "like."

250. perfringere: sc. *eam.*

251. algenti: ablative of present participle < *algeo*, "be chilly."

252. fragili . . . triumpho: "triumph over what is weaker [here, the 'weaker sex']."
uiros: Superbia thinks and speaks as a male; cf. *uirago* (194).

254. cornipedem: "horn-footed, hooved"; another poetic periphrasis for "horse."
laxis: "slackened."
temeraria: "hasty."

255. umbonis: < *umbo*, "shield."
equini: adjective, "horse-hide." Shields were covered with leather.

258. interciso . . . aequore: ablative absolute. *aequor:* "flat land, plain."

260. uersuta: "cunning."
opifex: "artificer."
praescia: "foreseeing" (+ genitive).

261. scrobibus: < *scrobis*, "hole."
uitiauerat: "had spoiled." Note the word-play on *uitium.*

262. hostili de parte: "on the enemy side."

263. mersa: < *mergo,* "sink."

265. oras: "edges."

266. superinposito . . . caespite: instrumental ablative.

268. opertum: neuter perfect participle < *operio*, used as noun, "hidden place."

269. furta: "trap."

270. praepete: < *praepes*, "headlong."

271. caecum: "hidden."
hiatum: "hole, pit."

272. prona: "head first."
inuoluitur: "is wrapped up, entangled," i.e., hangs on to the horse's neck to keep from falling off.

273. pectoris: that of the horse, which has fallen on top of her.
impressu: "pressure."

570-1. quid ... credat ... quidue ... notet: indirect deliberative questions dependent on *ignorans*.

571. letum: "deadly thing, destroyer."

572. lubricat: "causes to slip, makes unsteady."

uisus: here, "eyesight."

573. frendens: "gnashing her teeth."

Operatio: "Good Works, Generosity."

574. auxilio: dative of purpose.

capessit: "takes up."

575. gradu: "order, position."

duello: dative, archaic/poetical form of *bello*.

576. supersit: "remain." *Operatio* has been kept in reserve until the final battle. Cf. Matthew 19.20-1, where giving away one's possessions is the final step to perfection.

577. reiecerat: < *reicio*, "throw off."

578. induuiis: "outer garments."

fasce: < *fascis*, "burden."

leuarat = leuauerat: < *leuo*, "lighten."

579. talentis: The *talentum* was the largest currency unit in the ancient world. One talent was a large sum of money.

580. miserando: gerund (ablative of cause) < *miseror*, "take pity on" (here takes genitive, a poetic usage.)

inopum: genitive plural < *inops*, "poor, needy," here used as noun.

581. patrium: "ancestral, inherited."

bene prodiga: paradoxical, since *prodigus* generally has negative connotations.

582. loculos: "purses."

ditata: < *dito*, "enrich."

fidem: accusative of respect with *ditata*.

583. redituro faenore: ablative absolute. *faenore:* < *faenus*, "interest." Operatio is thinking of such texts as Matthew 19.29, which suggest the metaphor that renunciation now is an investment in the next world.

584. fulmen: "lighting-bolt," metaphorical for the sudden and alarming appearance of Operatio.

inpos: "lacking control over," with *mentis*, "out of her mind, demented."

586. certa: takes dependent infinitive.

restet: potential subjunctive.

587. calcatrix: "trampler"; feminine noun < *calcare*, "trample," coined by P. and occurring nowhere else.

mundi: objective genitive with *calcatrix*.

587-8. mundanis ... inlecebris: instrumental ablative dependent on *uicta*.

fatiscat: < *fatisco, -ere*, "fall apart, collapse."

588. spretoque ... auro: dative dependent on *inplicet*. **spreto:** < *sperno*, "scorn."

inplicet: < *inplico, -are*, "entangle."

589. inuadit: "attacks."

trepidam: sc. *Avaritiam*.

590. ulnarum: "arms," defining genitive.

591. exsanguem ... siccamque: The adjectives are proleptic, expressing the effect of the verb on its object.

gulam: "gullet."

ligantur: < *ligo*, "tighten."

592. lacertorum: genitive defining *uincla*; "the smith, a mighty man is he, ... and the muscles of his brawny arms are strong as iron bands" (Longfellow).

mentum: "chin."

faucibus artis: ablative of separation.

593. animam: means both "breath" and "life."

594. palpitat: "writhes."

aditu: "passage."

595. inclusam: with *mortem*.

596. illa: *Operatio*.

reluctanti: dative of present participle < *reluctor*, "struggle, resist."

calcibus: < *calx*, "heel."

instans: "treading on."

597. perfodit: "pierces."

costas: "ribs."

ilia: "groin."

anhela: "breathless."

598. extincto: "dead."

599. frusta: < *frustum*, "fragment, bit"; in apposition to *spolia* and also implied object of *dispergit* (602), "distributes."

rudis: genitive, "unrefined."

domus et plaga mundus: Supply *est*. Answers the question on *patria*. *plaga:* "region, zone."

715. ulterius: "further."

blasphemia: "blasphemies."

717. inpedit: "stops."

718. pollutam: "filthy."

rigida: ablative.

transfigens: "piercing, transfixing."

719. carpitur: "is torn to pieces."

bestia: "monster."

720. frustatim: adverb, "piecemeal, in pieces."

720-3. quod ... marinis: relative clauses of purpose.

721. edacibus: < *edax*, "voracious."

ultro: "spontaneously, freely."

722. caeno exhalante: ablative dependent on *inmundis*. *caeno:* "filth."

cloacis: dative of motion towards; "sewers."

723. trudat: "shove."

mandet: "entrust, give."

habere: infinitive of purpose.

724. discissum: < *discindo*, "tear apart."

foedis animalibus: dependent on *discissum*.

726-7. conpositis ... secundis ... bonis: The text of this obscure passage is probably corrupt. To make some sense, take as ablative absolute, with perfect participle *compositis* < *compono* "settle," *bonis* as neuter plural adjective used as noun, and *secundis* as a (rather redundant) adjective qualifying *bonis*.

rerum morumque: genitive dependent on *bonis*. *rerum:* "situation". *morum:* "character."

727. in commune: "in general."

tranquillae plebis: another genitive dependent on *bonis*.

ad unum: idiomatic for "altogether, without exception."

728. sensibus ...locatis: ablative absolute. *sensibus:* "the senses." P. reminds us that the location of the allegorical battle, on one level at least, is within the individual. The senses are posted to keep a look-out for approaching temptations. *locatis:* < *loco, -are,* "place."

ualli: "valley" < *uallis*.

statione: noun in apposition to *ualli*: "as a guard-post."

729. Our text has no line 729 because at this point the standard numbering follows a different text which is found in some late manuscripts.

730. tribunal: "speaking platform."

731. editiore: "higher" (comparative < *editus*).

tumulus: "hillock."

uertice acuto: ablative of description.

732. excitat: "raises up."

speculam: "look-out, watchtower" (accusative of purpose with *in*).

subiecta: "laid out below"; < *subicio*.

733. inoffenso: "unobstructed, uninterrupted."

734 hunc: modifies *apicem* (736).

sincera: "pure."

735. iuratae: "sworn."

sub: "in."

736. apicem: < *apex*, "peak."

737. par: neuter noun, "pair."

sibi: "to each other."

supreminet: "stands on top of" (+ direct object).

aequo: "equal."

738. iure potestatis: i.e., lawful authority.

aggere: "platform."

739. frequentes: proleptic, expressing the desired effect of the order.

740. alacres: Translate as adverb.

omnibus: "whole" (since *castris* is singular in meaning).

741. Mentis: P. reminds us again of the meaning of the allegory.

iners: predicative.

742. intercepta: < *intercipio*, "cut off."

sinu: ablative of place, "corner." P. thinks of soul/mind as distributed evenly throughout the body.

conceptacula: "hiding-places."

744. uelis: here, "tent-flaps."

reserantur: < *resero, -are*, "open."

carbasa: neuter plural, "canvas."

quis: "any," adjective modifying *habitator*.

745. marceat: < *marceo*, "laze."

operto: < *operio*; used as noun = "concealment."

stertens: < *sterto*, "snore."